AMAZING GRACE IN AMERICA

AMAZING GRACE IN AMERICA

Our Spiritual National Anthem

TEXT BY MARY ROURKE AND PICTURES COMPILED BY EMILY GWATHMEY

ANGEL CITY PRESS

ANGEL CITY PRESS, INC.

Published by Angel City Press
2118 Wilshire Boulevard, Suite 880
Santa Monica, California 90403
310.395.9982

FIRST PUBLISHED IN 1996 BY ANGEL CITY PRESS

1 3 5 7 9 10 8 6 4 2

FIRST EDITION

ISBN 1-883318-30-0

AMAZING GRACE IN AMERICA

Copyright © 1996 by Mary Rourke and Emily Gwathmey

Text copyright © 1996 by Mary Rourke

Designed by John Miller

LIBRARY OF CONGRESS CATALOGING-IN-PUBLICATION DATA

Rourke, Mary, 1949-
    Amazing grace in America : our spiritual national anthem / text by Mary Rourke ; pictures
compiled by Emily Gwathmey ; design by John Miller. — 1st ed.
        p.   cm.
    Includes bibliographical references.
    ISBN 1-883318-30-0
    1. Grace (Theology) 2. Amazing grace (Hymn)   I. Title.
BT761.2.R64 1996
234—dc20   96-25221
                                        CIP

DEDICATION

For my two mothers, Mary and Constance, both in heaven now.
And for my father, Clifford, who is also with God.

—M.R.

And for Janet

—E.G.

Contents

INTRODUCTION

The idea for this book came to me in a phone conversation with my friend Paddy Calistro, who is now also my publisher. At first the thought of writing about grace seemed impossible. Grace isn't something you can explain, I thought. It's something you have to experience. Still, I felt such an emotional pull toward the subject, I could not let it go.

Two years passed. From time to time Paddy and I talked again about grace and about how the hymn "Amazing Grace" seemed to explain it best. Neither of us would allow the idea to drift out of sight for long.

Then at last the timing was right. While I was earning my master's degree in religion, one of my professors, Margaret Farley, a Catholic nun, was renowned for her habit of saying yes to unconventional ideas that made sense to

IN OUR ONGOING QUEST TO CAPTURE GRACE IN ALL OF ITS MYSTERY, WE HAVE EVEN ATTEMPTED TO EMBODY IT OURSELVES. IN THE EARLY TWENTIETH CENTURY, WOMEN DRESSED AS GODDESSES TO IMITATE THE GRACES AND DANCED TO CELEBRATE LIFE.

her. One day I stood in her office explaining the concept of this book and she agreed to accept this as the written work for her course in moral theology. If grace were a doorway to opportunity, its name would be Sister Margaret.

During the months that I prepared to write the book, I often read the lyrics to John Newton's now famous hymn. On Sunday mornings I would look through the hymnal in whatever church I found myself. "Amazing Grace" was always there, in the most impressive leather-bound hymn books and the slightest paper mini-missals.

I was gaining courage.

Important as it was to understand what Newton wanted to say about grace, I had to find words for my own impressions. One example came quickly to mind. On a late summer afternoon as I got into my car, two men and a woman pushed me to the floor of the back seat. One planted his feet on me, one lurched my stick-shift sedan out of the parking lot, and one shouted orders. Four hours later I was tossed from the car and left on a busy street in Watts. I had been beaten and robbed.

But, by the grace of God, I had not been further molested. What is more, I was led to safety by complete strangers from the neighborhood. My friends Martha and Jeff Melvoin interrupted their honeymoon to pick me up. They took me to their home, where, in my terror, I stayed for more than a week — just me and the newlyweds.

Thanks to them, I met Susan and Jim Bell, who invited me to move in with them for the summer while I fought my fears. We are now as close as family. Since then I have never doubted that there is a God of mercy who has a plan for each of us. And that plan is carried out through the constant infusion of grace.

Now there are times when I feel grace move past me like a sudden wave of warmer air. I felt it as I worked on this book with Emily Gwathmey, who unearthed perfect pictures, John Miller who designed beautiful pages, my editor Jean Penn and the team at Angel City Press who guided us through the process.

Other times, I have seen grace coming toward me like a shower of light. When my mother died of leukemia, I was certain I saw her escorted to heaven. Her soul, her essential self, left the room, carried not by angels or saints, but by that good light, embracing her like the protective arms of the most loving parent.

Recently, I have started to recognize the grace that accompanies my failures. The first time it happened I was dumbfounded and, then, oddly delighted. I was about to have a conversation I dreaded, and I prayed that my visitor and I would have the grace to resolve our differences in a positive way. I imagined what ought to happen next. Well, it didn't. At best, we agreed to disagree. My idea of a happy ending is not necessarily the one I now expect. Grace will remind us that we are not in charge. Yet, I have come to find this enormously comforting. I would rather watch a divine master work things out than waste another minute trying to do it myself. In this way John Newton and I see eye to eye.

Mary Rourke
Pentecost, 1996

PART I

STATES
OF
GRACE

Often we own something of great beauty without knowing who made it. Over time we might invent a story to answer our questions about it, until we are sure we know the country, the year, the sort of person who gave it life. Later, if we learn the truth, we might be surprised by the ways it contradicts our fantasy. Many people have this feeling about the hymn "Amazing Grace."

As much as it speaks to our individual stories, this favorite spiritual seems also to express the story of our life together as Americans. Especially in this century, we have called upon it to comfort us as a nation at times when we long for relief from pain we all share. During foreign wars and periods of traumatic social unrest at home, "Amazing Grace" found a popular audience. World-famous gospel singers recorded it, and it climbed the pop charts. Civil rights leaders and

MARIAN ANDERSON, 1939

Perfection of movement is often the awe-inspiring embodiment of grace itself. More than the result of skill, coordination and practice, this kind of achievement requires a divine touch that allows one to soar beyond the ordinary. To explain this, Americans coined the phrase "grace in motion." Those who believe in God credit this Holy Being as the inspiration for their high performance and acknowledge that God-given grace affords their success.

antiwar activists gave us soulful versions. Each time the hymn rose to prominence, it settled deeper into our collective soul.

Perhaps there is something in the simple word *grace*. It has a power and a mystery that the hymn transmits. We sing of amazing grace and we feel reassured that all will be well, even if the solution depends on powers beyond our control.

Every major religion of the world sees grace as a gift from the divine. For Jews, to be graced is to be blessed beyond all expectations. The natural response is thanksgiving and praise.

Christians believe the ultimate gift of grace is the salvation of souls. This is the highest expression of God's love for us. Saving grace frees a soul from sin and opens the way to an eternity in heaven.

Muslims include grace among the ninety-nine holy attributes of Allah, along with perfection and purity. Tibetan Buddhists pray for the gift of compassionate grace. Hindus have a marvelous expression: "The winds of grace are constantly blowing, but we must open our sails."

Early in the twentieth century Gandhi showed us how to live with sails open to this mystical wind. He led India on a course of nonviolent resistance to achieve social reform. His way demanded a radical trust in the reality of grace. As they fought to free India from British rule, Gandhi and his followers did not raise a hand against the soldiers who beat them and even murdered them. In the end Gandhi's way of peaceful resistance prevailed. His country gained its independence.

People who believe in God consider every grace to be a gift from this sacred source. Big things — cosmic order, peace, health, food and shelter — are ours by the merciful grace of God. Smaller things — harmony in our homes, satisfying work — are signs of grace. Good things — vacations, birthday parties, the scent of roses — come to us by the grace of God. Even difficult things — illness, the loss of a loved one, plans that fail — bring grace. Often, such hardships inspire kindness, forgiveness and healing.

At times grace strikes like lightning. More often, though, it is like a cosmic safety net or a sacred web that upholds all of life. This is grace at its most subtle. It is the stuff of everyday life and keeps things rolling along.

People attuned to ordinary encounters with grace see them as something remarkable. They may come to value these encounters more than they do the huge and dramatic moments in life.

Marianne Williamson is a spiritual healer who has spent many years working with AIDS patients in Los Angeles. She sees life-changing events at the bedsides of the dying. But when she recalls a moment of grace in her own life, something else comes to mind. "When I have felt graced, it was obvious to me that the universe made right something I made wrong," she says. This sort of redemption is appreciated most when it affects our personal relationships. If we say something we wish we had not said, or fail to keep a promise, or lose our temper, we may feel as though there is no grace to be found. "Then," says Williamson, "it's as if a hand reaches down and touches a deep place in my soul, to change things. Grace always seems to involve my weakness, but it moves me toward strength."

Sometimes the grace we meet in everyday life reminds us that ordinary events are quite extraordinary. Williamson, expressing a feeling many parents have had, remembers a particularly powerful encounter of this sort: "It was the first time I laid eyes on my child," she says. A farmer might have a similar feeling while looking out over a ripe field — or even a backyard patch of tomatoes. No farmer would dare to take for granted the sunlight, heat and rain essential for a good harvest. Every new crop reminds us all of how we depend on the sustaining grace that keeps nature on course.

As often as grace lifts our spirits in good times, it carries us through hardships. Brother Arnold, a member of the Shaker community of Sabbathday Lake in New Gloucester, Maine, is reminded of this at Sunday meetings, when people give testimony about the joys and disappointments of their lives. "Grace is the understanding that we live in God's love," he says. Our job is to trust that God's love will sustain us no matter what.

Amazing grace! How sweet the sound, That saved a wretch like me!

In the hymn "Amazing Grace," we are honest about ourselves. Grace saved a wretch like me, we sing. At our lowest points, grace will find us. In 1996

I once was lost, but now am found, Was blind, but now I see!

Tommy Morrison, a world champion boxer, learned that he was HIV positive. The shock forced him to look back over his past. He was raised in Missouri, the child of religious parents. But when he moved to Kansas City for the sake of his career, he gave up his religious practices. He was busy chasing success and fame. Women spun through his life so fast that he could not remember their names. "I used boxing as an excuse to live a life I knew I shouldn't be living," he states. "I had lots of money, and I was the most miserable guy I knew."

Still, Morrison admits, his life as a champion boxer seemed glamorous and exciting. He believes he was not strong enough to leave it behind. "God knew it would be hard for me to give up that life, so he took me out of the sport," he says.

His moment of grace came wrapped in a painful truth. But Morrison is slowly absorbing all the meaning he can from it. He moved from Kansas City to a ranch near a small town where life revolves around being a good neighbor. He makes appearances at high schools, teaching young people about the dangers of AIDS. "I want to live a certain way and help people," he says of his future. He accepted what grace he could find in a difficult situation; now he will use it to make life better for others.

And what of the times when the absence of grace is extreme to the point of pain, even death? We have all wondered why terrible things happen if there is grace or God, or both. Great philosophers have pondered this question and come to similar conclusions: to say that there is a divine source of life is not to say this source prevents the world's troubles. Part of what it means to be human is to make choices. And evil, as well as good, is a choice. When people go against the good, it brings pain and sometimes violence. Then our greatest comfort is in knowing that grace does not disappear.

Americans were reminded of this by the Oscar-winning movie *Schindler's List*. It portrays the true story of a wealthy European businessman who sets up a factory in Poland where he can operate at lower costs. Oskar Schindler arrives in Poland just as Hitler sets out to destroy the Jews. When Schindler sees the Polish Jews being marched off to death camps and hears stories of mass murder, he finds a new mission: he hires Jewish workers for his factory to save them.

He uses every ruse, including bribes and threats, to convince the Nazis to let him keep his employees. He pretends that it is only for business reasons. And through his commitment, he does save hundreds of lives.

Schindler's List shows us how the winds of grace continue to blow even in the face of evil. Fortunately for so many, Oskar Schindler opened his sails to receive it. In the face of terrible injustice, he was a force for good. That is not to say the man was born a saint. He liked his money, his fine clothes, his fancy car. Often as not, grace breaks into lives that we do not particularly admire — imperfect lives, like our own.

'Twas grace that taught my heart to fear, And grace my fears relieved

In the early 1970s Chuck Colson served as special counsel to President Richard Nixon. He was said to have more power than members of the President's cabinet. His office, with its massive carved wood door, was right next to the President's. In every political battle Nixon faced, from nominating Supreme Court justices to quieting student protests against the Vietnam War, Colson was the troubleshooter. People started to call him Nixon's hatchet man.

Colson burned out. He quit some months before the Watergate trials that brought about the fall of Nixon's presidency. He wanted a slower-paced life.

Setting up a private practice, he began building a clientele. One name on his list was a longtime acquaintance, Tom Phillips, head of Raytheon, an electronics manufacturer. Phillips invited him home for dinner. Colson still remembers the scene:

"I was part of the cynical East Coast establishment," he says, "but I felt an emptiness in my life. My friend Tom seemed completely different from the person I once knew. I asked him what had changed. He said he had met Jesus Christ and embraced him as his personal savior.

"I almost fell off my chair."

Cynicism gave way to curiosity as the evening unfolded. At one point, Phillips opened the book *Mere Christianity* by C.S. Lewis and began to read

How precious did that grace appear, The hour I first believed!

Visages Chrétiens Cévenols
(lecture de la Bible)

ACOMA INDIANS
FRASHERS FOTO - POMONA

aloud a passage on the destructive powers of pride: "A proud man is always looking down on things and people; and of course, as long as you are looking down, you cannot see something that is above you."

Colson still considers that night as the turning point in his life. "Reading from C.S. Lewis was a pure act of grace," he believes. Of all the authors in the world, Phillips chose the one who spoke to Colson's soul. At the end of the evening, Colson says, "I went out to start my car and I couldn't. I was crying too hard."

His night of grace did not release him from punishment for his illegal activities while serving as Nixon's special counsel. Colson was charged with obstructing justice in the Watergate case, and he went to prison. But in 1975, after he finished serving time, Colson built a prison fellowship ministry to help other inmates. It continues nationwide.

Colson saw the light — theologians call this *illumination* — and it showed him that he was wrong. After illumination, though, the road to change requires many more encounters with grace. Old, familiar ways seem easier, even if they lead to misery. No doubt it is a good thing that grace is always in the wind. Clearly, someone always needs it.

When grace shows us a painful sight, it also brings forgiveness. You could say it brings a second chance. Los Angeles Lakers basketball star Earvin "Magic" Johnson got a second chance in 1991. He shocked the nation when he announced that he was HIV positive and would quit basketball at the top of his game. Two days later he learned that the news was even worse. His wife, Earleatha "Cookie" Johnson, was carrying their baby. Johnson was well aware of the risks. His wife could be infected. His baby could be born with AIDS. But neither of these things happened. Mother and baby were spared, and Earvin Johnson III remains healthy. Magic Johnson learned about the grace that brings a second chance.

While grace can strike like a warrior at times, more often it comes as a messenger of healing and peace. Sometimes the messenger is an ordinary person. We are all grace-bearers at times. In January 1982 a plane skidded into the

The Lord has promised good to me, His word my hope secures. He will my shield and portion be As long as life endures.

Potomac River near Washington, D.C. One man, Arland D. Williams Jr., helped other passengers reach the lifeline sent down by a rescue helicopter while he treaded the icy waters. More than once he had the choice to save himself, but he never did. He saved the lives of others but lost his own.

Through many dangers, toils, and snares, I have already come. 'Tis

In whatever way grace breaks in, it changes a life for the better. People who would not call themselves saints or sinners can find themselves caught up in the most powerful waves of grace. That is the story of Luis Abreu. A Cuban bus driver, he found a message in a bottle. It had been sent by the students of Harbor Day School in Corona del Mar, California. The students became Abreu's pen pals. As if that was not unlikely enough for one lifetime, he went on to win a lottery in Cuba, which gave him the right to a U.S. visa. Abreu was determined to come to America, but he did not have any money.

His pen pals and their teacher, Judy d'Albert, swung into action. Next thing he knew, Luis and his wife Miriam, had immigrated to the United States. They had a place to stay and enough money to get them started. "It was a miracle," Abreu said again and again in those first few weeks. "There were two hundred thousand names in the lotto; five thousand won. That was God's grace."

Not all stories have happy endings. For every Luis Abreu there is an Arland Williams Jr. Some say this is the work of fate or chance. But others see sacred thumbprints pressed upon every person's story, no matter how it ends. This may help explain our great affection for the hymn "Amazing Grace." We sing it and we are reminded of our constant need for love and support, our unending quest for guidance, our inborn sense that there is a life force greater than our own — and our deep desire to find a home in the arms of this tender, loving parent.

John Newton, who wrote the hymn, might not fit the image most people have of him. The author of America's beloved spiritual was not himself an American. He lived in eighteenth-century England, and he was not the saintly per-

grace has brought me safe thus far, And grace will lead me home.

son some might imagine. Newton was a slave trader, a libertine and a self-professed philanderer. But that all changed one terrifying night at sea when a winter storm nearly sank his ship. The winds of grace were blowing, and, for once, Newton opened his own sails.

Later he became a minister and wrote his autobiographical hymn to commemorate his own dramatic conversion. By then he saw that he was blessed by endless encounters with grace. Still, it was that first life-changing gust of grace that made the lasting impression.

If we believe, as he did, that the world is filled with bounty and blessings, we begin to see them all around us. A life that others might regard as insignificant becomes a life guided by the divine. If we watch for it, we notice all the more often that grace is flowing past us. Do we dare open our sails?

John
Newton's
Story

AMAZING GRACE, HOW SWEET THE SOUND, THAT SAVED A WRETCH LIKE ME!

John Newton probably wrote "Amazing Grace" sometime in the 1760s, when he was well into his forties and curate of Olney parish in Buckinghamshire, near London. By then, he knew from hard experience what it was like to be at the brink of disaster, to be battered by disease, to be alone and in need of help, and to feel the tender mercy of divine intervention. He also knew quite a lot about grace. He saw it as a many-faceted gift that came from God. At times it compared with a thunderbolt, loud enough to command undivided attention and show him how he needed to change his life. At other times it compared to a steady flow of energy that sent him the strength to resist temptation and do what was right. At its most welcome, grace felt like a wave of good luck. Sparkling coincidences and happy endings proved to be moments of grace once Newton recognized them. Somehow he conveys both the need for grace and the comfort it brings in his beloved hymn. After two centuries, "Amazing Grace" still has a way of saying all that needs to be said — in

40 John Newton's Story

the battered times as well as in the blessed.

Most of us hear "Amazing Grace" for the first time in church. It has been included in American hymnals for about 200 years. However, with its power to soothe and reassure listeners, to express both gratitude and remorse, the hymn could not be contained by church walls. It quickly found its way to more public gatherings. These days many family reunions, camp sing-alongs and small-town covered-dish suppers are considered incomplete without it.

Newton himself helps explain our deep attachment to his spiritual. In a sense his story is like so many others. There is the classic battle between the spirit and the flesh, between desire and virtue, between career and the higher calling. But in Newton's case, the difference is that each significant moment came wrapped in melodrama. A prolific writer, he penned his own full descriptions of these many twists and turns.

The broad strokes of his life are these: he was born in London in July 1725. At the age of six he lost his mother and spent his teens struggling to get along with his stern and remote father. He entered the slave trade when he was twenty and nearly drowned three years later during a severe storm at sea in March 1748. That storm was a turning point in his life. Within two years he had taken steps to change careers, reclaim the religion his mother had taught him to cherish and marry his childhood sweetheart.

Following his ordination at thirty-nine, in 1764, he gave forty-three years to the ministry. Still, he did not begin to speak out against the evils of slavery until he was in his mid-fifties. First he spoke from the pulpit. Later he testified before England's Privy Council. Finally, he saw the soul-destroying system abolished in his own country in 1807. That year, at eighty-two, he died in peace. A frightful injustice he once supported had been outlawed at last.

Newton described many important events of his young life in a series of letters, *An Authentic Narrative*, published in 1764, that he wrote as an application for ordination. His memories of childhood recollect a boy caught in the crossfire between his parents' conflicting plans for him. His father pushed him toward financial success while his mother pulled him toward spiritual enlightenment.

John Newton

'Twas grace that taught my heart to fear, And grace my fears relieved.
How precious did that grace appear, The hour I first believed!

His father, Commander John Newton, was a merchant seaman who expected his son to follow in his footsteps. Elizabeth Newton envisioned her son as a minister, and she invested all her efforts in nurturing him toward that end. In those early years, his father was away from home for a year or more at a time, leaving Newton to his mother's influence. "The tender mercies of God toward me were manifest in the first moment of my life," he wrote in *An Authentic Narrative*. "I was born as it were in his house, and dedicated to Him in my infancy." Of his mother's devotion, he noted: "I was her only child and as she was of a weak constitution and a retired temper, almost her whole employment was the care of my education."

By the age of four he could read, and he had memorized passages from the Bible. At six he was studying Latin. His mother had barely set him on the road to the ministry when she died of tuberculosis. Her death came less than two weeks before his seventh birthday.

The child, deeply religious and accustomed to a close relationship with the divine, suddenly found himself cut off from his main source of spiritual instruction. Without his mother, Newton's enthusiasm for the moral path all but faded from memory. He received little encouragement from his father, who valued life's more bankable resources. Of the days that followed his mother's death, Newton wrote very little. "My father was then at sea (he was a commander in the Mediterranean trade at the time): he came home the following year, and soon after married again." His brief account of such a dramatic change suggests a vast emotional distance from his father. Soon after the commander's second marriage, the boy was sent off to boarding school. A stern headmaster there all but broke his spirit and dulled his interest in learning.

After two difficult years, Commander Newton removed his eleven-year-old son from school and took the boy to sea with him. In the rough company of merchant sailors, Newton wrote, he began cursing and indulging his impatient nature.

Two near-death experiences in those early years reformed him, but only temporarily. At about age twelve he fell from a horse, his head barely missed a garden stake hidden in a hedge. It was perhaps his first memory of an encounter with grace — a gift of merciful protection that he had not asked for or earned. "I

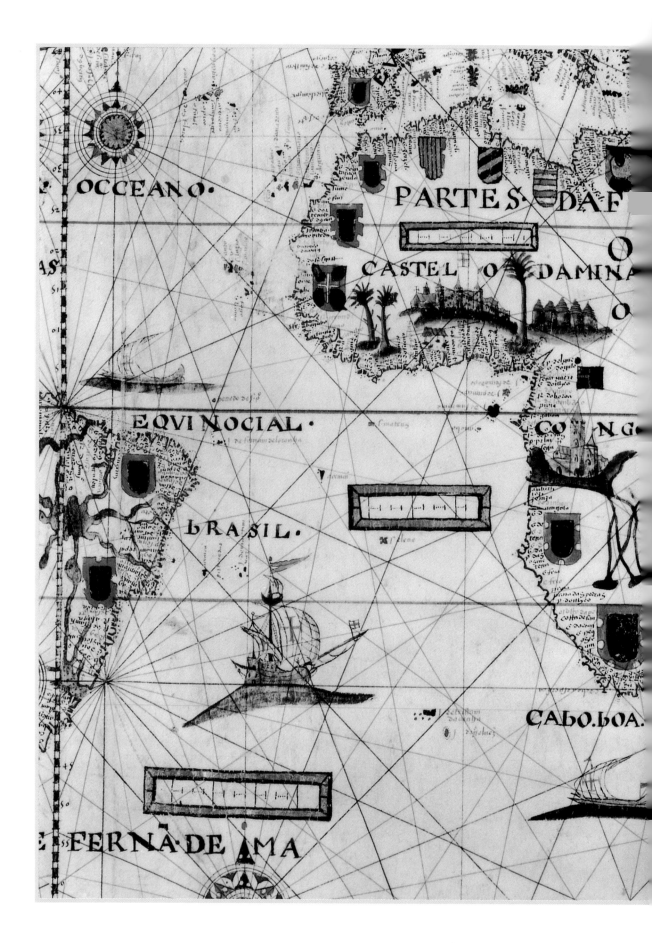

OCCEANO·

PARTES·DA F

CASTEL O DAMNA

EQVINOCIAL·

CONGO

BRASIL·

CABO·BOA·

FERNÃ·DE MA

IERVSALEM

ACHINA

CA

MARROXo

LO

S. E IOA

CEILAM

MAR·DA·INDIA

SAN·LOVRENCO·

SPERAÇA·

DOMINGOS·
TEIXEIRA
1573

got no hurt, but could not avoid taking notice of a gracious providence in my deliverance; for had I fallen upon the stake, I had inevitably been killed." His gratitude was short-lived. "I presently broke off from my profane practices and appeared quite altered; but it was not long before I declined again," he recalled.

Not many years later, Newton was saved from another near fatality. He was supposed to meet a friend and tour a warship anchored in the Thames. They planned to take a small boat from shore. "We had agreed to go on a man-of-war (I think it was on a Sunday) but I providentially came too late; the boat was overset, and he and several others were drowned," Newton wrote. At the time he saw this tragedy as a frightening coincidence. Years later he recognized it as another experience of heaven's mercy. By the time he wrote about it, he had come to believe that grace actually does exist. There were many long and difficult years between boyhood and maturity when he believed no such thing.

By age fifteen, Newton's early religious experiences and his later rebellions had turned his inner world to chaos. He would swing from devout prayerfulness to angry rejection of every religious teaching and practice. Trips to sea with his father imposed an external order, but he missed his mother's tender guidance. Commerce and career won out over spirit and soul. Still, it was a halfhearted choice for Newton. He respected his father as "a man of remarkable good sense, and great knowledge of the world." But, he added, "I was always in fear when before him, and therefore he had the less influence."

Despite his stern manner, "the old gentleman," as Newton later referred to his father, did care. He found his wayward son one respectable job after another on merchant ships owned by his friends. This intervention did not help. Teenage Newton was always overstaying shore leave, writing nasty limericks about his superiors and stirring up the other sailors with his testy attitude. Whenever young John got in trouble, his determined father stepped in to set things right.

At the age of seventeen, on his way to his next assignment at sea, Newton received a letter from his mother's friends George and Mary Catlett, urging him to visit them in Chatham, a country town due east of London. Mary Catlett and Elizabeth Newton had been schoolmates. When Elizabeth fell ill, the

By age fifteen, Newton's deeply religious mother had died and his business-minded father became the dominating influence in his life. Young Newton vacillated between being a devout Christian, born of his mother's teachings, and an angry agnostic. He struggled between commerce and career on one hand, spirit and soul on the other.

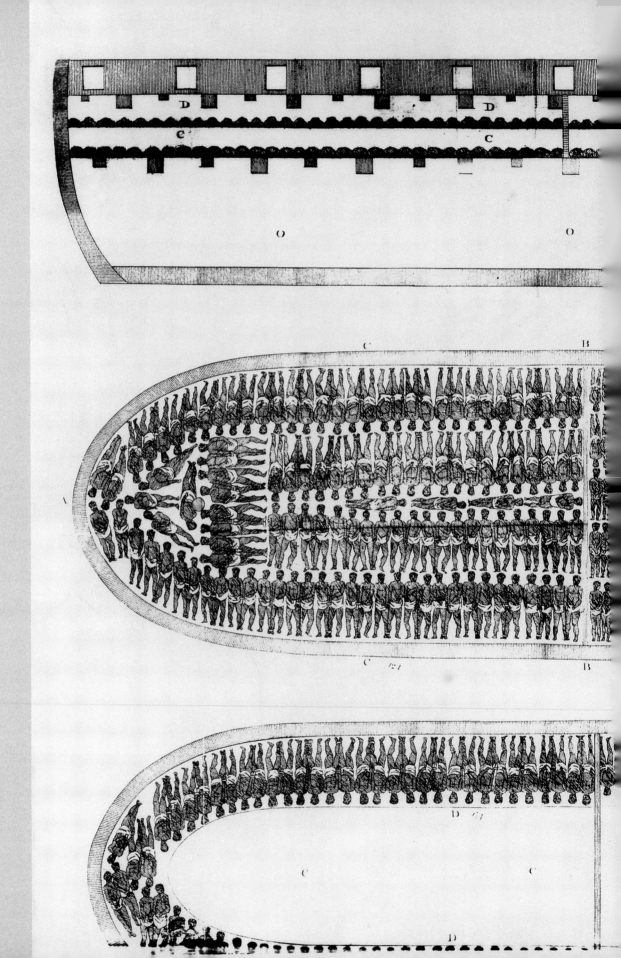

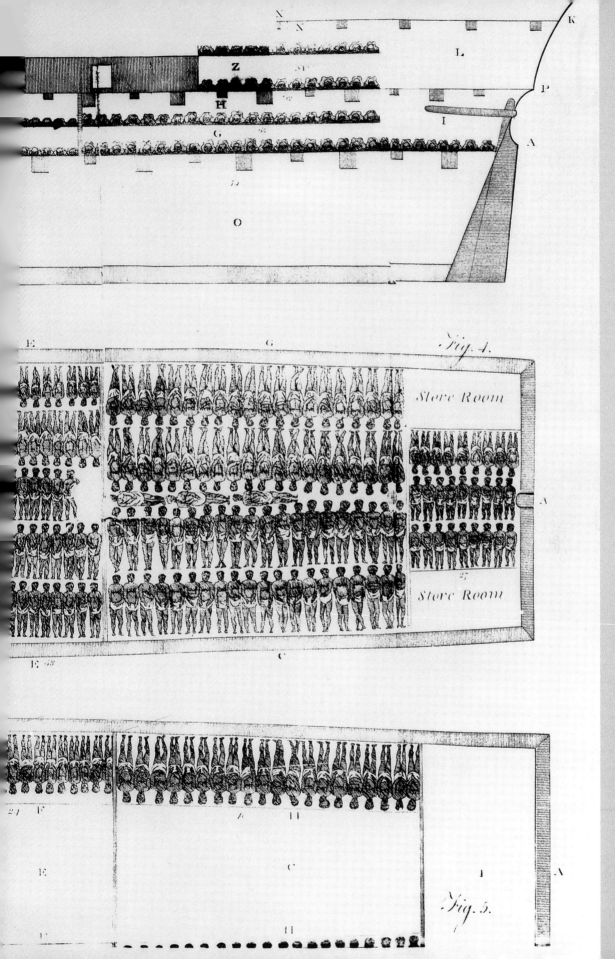

Fig. 4.

Store Room

Store Room

Fig. 5.

Catletts brought her to Chatham and cared for her until her death.

There were five children in the Catlett family, including Mary, named after her mother and nicknamed Polly. She was four years younger than Newton, and he was drawn to her from the start. Polly was shy and known for her sweet singing voice. It was Christmas time; the family was warm and inviting. Newton extended his planned three-day visit to three weeks. By then, his ship had sailed and he had fallen in love.

Newton's voyages continued nonetheless. As was the custom for all merchant seaman, the young man traveled for more than a year at a time. From the start George Catlett did not approve of Newton's affection for Polly. The young couple could correspond only because one of Polly's aunts secretly passed their letters back and forth. However, Newton found Polly's letters to be distressingly noncommittal. It would pain him, when he was at home in England, to learn that she had enjoyed herself with friends while he was away. Apparently his budding career as a seaman did more than starve his spiritual growth. It put a real crimp in his love life as well.

In 1743 England was on the verge of war with France and, like many young sailors, John Newton was pressed into military service. On the decks of the *HMS Harwich*, Newton's slide from grace accelerated. He met a sailor named James Mitchell, who introduced him to the "free thinker" philosophy. Mitchell taught that every man had to look out for himself and not worry too much about how he treated others. In his view, moral standards were meaningless, since there was no heaven or hell.

It was perfect ammunition for an impressionable young rebel. Free thinking gave Newton permission to cut ties with the virtuous life he found difficult to follow. "I had not the least fear of God before my eyes nor (so far as I remember) the least sensibility of conscience," he wrote. He was never farther from realizing his mother's dream for him.

Military life was strict and did not agree with the undisciplined young man. He deserted ship when the *Harwich* docked at Plymouth, England. Then, for perhaps the first time in his adult life, Newton was held responsible for his actions. The cap-

The Lord has promised good to me, His word my hope secures.
He will my shield and portion be As long as life endures.

IN AFRICA, NEWTON FOUND WORK IN THE LUCRATIVE SLAVE TRADE, A
LEGAL BUSINESS AT THE TIME. ONLY THE QUAKERS, THE RELIGIOUS
COMMUNITY WITH MEMBERS IN ENGLAND AND AMERICA, CONDEMNED IT.

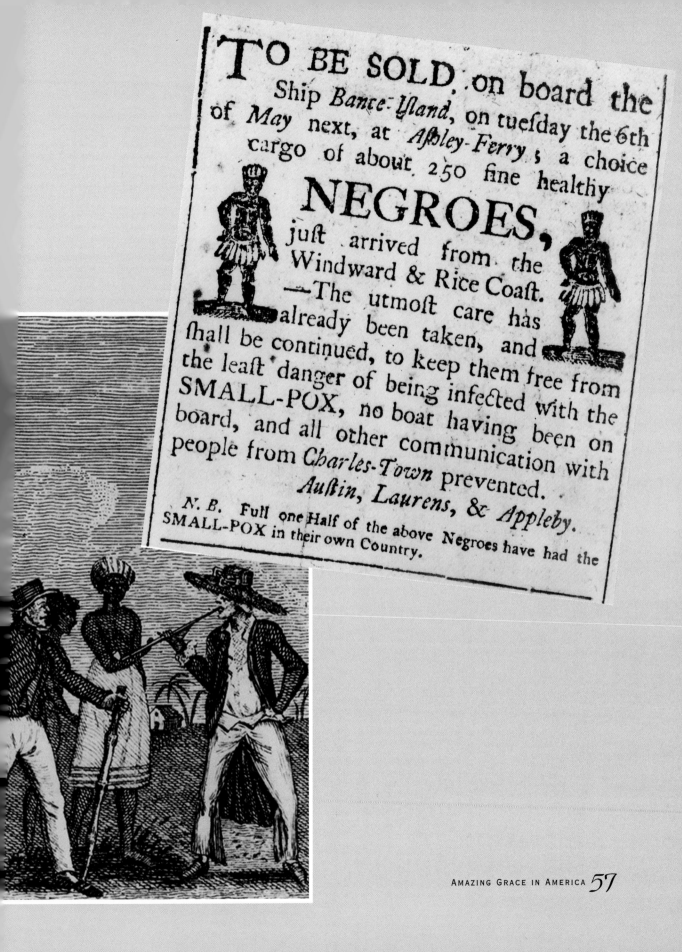

TO BE SOLD on board the Ship *Bance-Island*, on tuesday the 6th of *May* next, at *Ashley-Ferry*; a choice cargo of about 250 fine healthy NEGROES, just arrived from the Windward & Rice Coast. —The utmost care has already been taken, and shall be continued, to keep them free from the least danger of being infected with the SMALL-POX, no boat having been on board, and all other communication with people from *Charles-Town* prevented.

Austin, Laurens, & Appleby.

N. B. Full one Half of the above Negroes have had the SMALL-POX in their own Country.

tain had him whipped and stripped of his midshipman's rank. He was deeply humiliated, which only encouraged his defiant streak. Not long after he was publicly shamed, he learned that the commander of a trading ship bound for Africa would board the *Harwich*, looking for volunteers to leave military service and join his commercial venture. The captain of the *Harwich* allowed Newton to leave.

Once in Africa he looked for work in the lucrative slave trade. By then he was cut off from family, friends and religious faith. He forgot the honorable character his mother envisioned for him. Adrift without a plan, his head filled with a self-serving view of life, Newton made it all the more difficult for divine intervention to break through. He set up this spiritual blockade at the very time he most needed moral support.

It was 1745, Newton was twenty, and he met a man he referred to later only as Mr. Clow. Clow was a slave trader who hired Newton to help expand his business. They built a temporary prison, called a factory, to house the African captives they had traded for rum or rice. Clow collected these future slaves from professional kidnappers as well as from the African chiefs who regularly invaded weaker tribes and bartered their conquests for Clow's goods. He shipped his human cargo to England and America to be sold. Half of a typical shipment consisted of women and children.

Slave trading was a legal business. Only the Quakers, the religious community with members in America and England, condemned it. For Newton, it was simply a way to a rich man's future. No pangs of conscience kept him from abusing his captives as freely as the next man. But his body belied his depravity. His physical well-being deteriorated in a way that matched his moral decay when he developed a fever that left him too weak to work. His employer went to sea without him. While her husband was away, Clow's wife suddenly turned against Newton. It is not exactly clear why. Perhaps Newton's arrogant manner offended her, as it already had offended so many other people. She shut him into a slave hut, along with the African captives. What little food Newton ate during those weeks came from his fellow captives. These kidnap victims shared their own small portions with him. The tenderness he longed for came to him from the very peo-

THE **VOYAGE OF THE SABLE VENUS** (PAGE 59), USING AS A REFERENCE BOTTICELLI'S FAMOUS **BIRTH OF VENUS**, ROMANTICIZED THE TERRIBLE REALITY OF SLAVERY. FOR A TIME, NEWTON CLOSED HIS EYES TO THE CRUELTY OF THE SYSTEM. THEN, AT HIS LOWEST POINT, HE FOUND FORGIVENESS AND CHARITY FROM THE VERY PEOPLE HE KIDNAPPED. SOME COMPARE SUCH GRACE BEARERS TO ANGELS.

ple he intended to sell as slaves. Yet at the time, this did not cause him any shame.

Finally he recovered his health and sailed on Clow's next excursion. It proved to be worse than being imprisoned by the slave trader's wife. Clow chained Newton below deck and left him for days while he went by longboat to collect slaves from the villages along the narrow rivers. Newton does not explain why. More than demonstrating Clow's cruelty, the incident illustrates the quality of person attracted to Newton's line of work.

Faced with the absence of grace, he did not stop to consider why the world so needs it. Instead, he passed along the cruelty he met. To his way of thinking, the slaves were no better than laboring animals, to be used and abused without regret. It was a graceless existence that led him further and further from all spiritual moorings.

He managed to leave Clow behind for a new job as the warden of another factory, in Gambia. Not long after that he was rescued by one of Commander Newton's friends, Captain Joseph Manesty of the trade ship *Greyhound*. Manesty offered to take Newton to England and treated him like an honored guest when they set sail. But the kindness of others was not something Newton seemed able to accept at that time in his life. He did not return the captain's favors with gratitude, or even respect. Instead, he spent his time preaching the free-thinker's code and drinking rum on deck when he should have been sleeping.

Clearly, subtle attempts to awaken the soul of this hard-bitten sailor were wasted. No simple act of kindness could reach him. He needed something bolder. And so it came, in the darkness of March 10, 1748, on his voyage home with Manesty. "I went to bed that night in my usual security and indifference, but was awakened from a sound sleep by the force of a violent sea which broke on board us; so much of it came down below as filled the cabin I lay in with water."

He was sure his life was over, and there would be no merciful God to lead him home to heaven. Still, he heard himself call out for mercy, which surprised him. He thought he had convinced himself there was no divine source of all life. "I waited with fear and impatience to receive my inevitable doom," he wrote of the experience. Somehow, the ship stayed afloat. After hours of bailing

The Lord's Prayer.

Our Father, which art in Heaven,
hallowed be Thy Name.

Amazing grace! How sweet the sound,

That saved a wretch like me!

I once was lost, but now am found,

Was blind, but now I see!

'Twas grace that taught my heart to fear,

And grace my fears relieved.

How precious did that grace appear,

The hour I first believed!

The Lord has promised good to me,

His word my hope secures.

He will my shield and portion be

As long as life endures.

Through many dangers, toils and snares,

I have already come.

'Tis grace has brought me safe thus far,

And grace will lead me home.

water, Newton took the helm. As he steered a course to nowhere, his mind wandered across the events of his recent life. The memories disturbed him. "I concluded at first that my sins were too great to be forgiven." His former religious convictions, his brushes with death, the many signs of a merciful parent of divine degree — and his cavalier responses — shamed him.

He didn't dare to pray. He was sure God would not listen. But on the second day of the storm, Manesty told him that the boat was clear of water and might actually reach land. At that moment Newton saw the first gleam of hope in many unhappy years. He thought God might still remember him after all.

The condition of the ship itself did not inspire confidence. Pigs, sheep and poultry had been washed overboard in the storm. Casks of provisions were beaten to pieces. All that was left on board were a few dried cod. But he and the battered crew proceeded, clinging to life "with an alternate prevalence of hope and fear."

It was fear that led Newton to call upon God. Still, he was not sure he knew whom he was calling. He had to begin again, reviewing all that he had been taught and reflecting on all that happened in his tempestuous life. "My leisure time was chiefly employed in reading and meditating on the scriptures, and praying to the Lord for mercy and instruction," he wrote of the quiet days after the storm. Four weeks later, the *Greyhound* landed at Lough Swilly, on Ireland's northwest coast.

"About this time I began to believe and know there is a God, who hears and answers prayers," Newton recalled.

His life had changed forever.

I once was lost, but but now am found, Was blind but now I see!

A massive infusion of grace struck John Newton on that stormy night at sea. A permanent shift, from sinner to saint, should follow such a drama. The words of his famous hymn tell of this conversion. Once lost, he felt he was found at last. Not only found, but forgiven and saved from death.

The rest of Newton's life, however, does not unfold in such tidy fashion. Once his eyes were opened and he glimpsed the virtuous life, he needed more grace word, has declar'd next to impossible, it pleased the richness of the Divine Grace to effect in me; Who can prescribe to the efficacy or the freedom of the Holy Spirit? Why was I so long spar'd, & at length brought to a timely sense of my condition, when many who never sinn'd against half so much conviction have been cut off without hope? Lord I adore in silence! the reason is unknown to me, but one thing I know, that whereas I was blind, I now see in some measure, enlighten'd by the Sun of Righteousness. I see the lost & undone condition I must have been in without Christ, I see a merit & sufficiency in him, to atone for all my Offences, to make up all my infirmities, & to preserve my soul (that now desires to trust entirely in Him) from ever so basely forsaking him again. I see a real beauty & consonancy in all his commands, & I see an exceeding & eternal weight of glory laid up for those that in his faith, fear & love endeavour to keep them; the gift of his goodness, & the purchase of his Blood. And I embrace & believe with my whole heart, this most faithful saying, & worthy of all acceptation, that He came voluntarily into the world to seek & to save the chief of sinners, not excepting even such a hardned wretch as me. O my Soul praise the Lord! O gracious Saviour I beseech thee to take care of thy own work, suffer me not to deceive myself, & say peace when there is no true peace, nor let me receive thy grace in vain, but enable me to approve my self thy Disciple indeed, by bearing much fruit to thy Honour and Glory, & the manifestation of thy exceedingly abundant mercy I have experienced. Amen — Amen

Thursday y'e 13th August. Yesterday afternoon arriv'd in safety at Sierra-Leon, with every body well, having not met with the least accident, & hardly the least inconvenience upon the passage: for which I desire to return my hearty thanks to my gracious Preserver; as I can only have recourse to his mercy when things happen wrong, so I ascribe it wholly to his goodness that they have at present prov'd so far agreeable to my hopes & wishes. Lord grant that I may endeavour to show my gratitude by my obedience; & as I am going to engage in a more active course of life than of late, let me begin with begging thy blessing upon my undertakings, & give me grace that I may not thro' the hurry of
business

to help him live it. From that stormy hour when he first believed to the last, worthy battle he fought against slavery, his story is a lesson in how grace enters our lives time and again if we let it. Each time, it brings what we need to keep us on course.

When he returned home, he knew he wanted to accomplish two things. First he planned to ask his father for forgiveness. He was able to see for the first time that he had returned years of parental concern with careless ingratitude. By the time he arrived in London, however, Commander Newton had sailed for Fort York in the Hudson Bay to serve as governor. Newton never saw him again. After some years away, the "old gentleman" planned to return to England, but in a freak accident he was seized by a cramp while swimming and drowned. Until his death, however, he and his son corresponded.

Newton's second goal was to propose marriage to Polly. Upon seeing her, though, words failed him. Instead, he proposed by letter. "Her answer, though penned with abundance of caution, satisfied me," he remembered. "I collected from it that she was free from any other engagement and not unwilling to wait the event of the voyage I had undertaken." The voyage he refers to was another trip to Africa. Manesty offered him the slave ship *Brownlow* to command, and Newton accepted. He and Polly married in 1750, eight years after they first met. The groom was twenty-five years old, the bride twenty-one.

For five years after they wed, Newton continued as a slave trader, doing business with men who brought him African captives for sale. Once he purchased them, Newton gave each a number and never referred to them by name. Entries in his journal from 1750 and 1751 describe inhuman conditions. He packed these men and women on his ship as if they were cargo, chaining them in place. Forms of discipline he chose would qualify as torture today.

One thing, however, had changed. Newton had a new image of the man he wanted to be. Unlike earlier flashes of inspiration, this one took hold. He prayed for the strength to be faithful, and it came. He even began to lead his men in Sunday worship services.

By slave trade standards, an honorable man was one who treated captives as human beings, rather than beating and violating them. Later, Newton

How precious did that grace appear, The hour I first believed!

FOR CHRISTIANS, THE MOMENT OF CONVERSION IS EUPHORIC.
THEY BELIEVE THAT, AFTERWARD, THE CONSTANT FLOW OF GRACE
LEADS A PERSON HOME.

admitted to deep pangs of conscience. Nonetheless, he could not admit to the immorality of his profession while he still practiced it. "I was sometimes shocked with an employment that was perpetually conversant with chains, bolts and shackles," he eventually confessed. "In this view I had often petitioned in my prayers that the Lord in his own time would be pleased to fix me in a more humane calling."

In those years as he traveled from England to Africa, Newton met Alexander Clunie. He was a British trader in gold and ivory, not slaves, and a deeply religious man.

Sometimes grace comes to us through another person who brings what we need at the time. Often, that person is not even aware of it. Clunie was a grace-bearer for Newton. Over the years, he would reappear and bring opportunity each time. At home in England, several years after they first met, Clunie introduced Newton to the Anglican church leaders who assisted him toward ordination.

At about that time it became clear to Newton that Captain Manesty was another grace-bearer in his life. Manesty rescued Newton from his first disastrous year in Africa. Then he made Newton captain of his own ship. In the summer of 1755, he found Newton a job that rescued him from the slave trade. With Manesty's help, Newton obtained a position as a customs officer in Liverpool, England. He had stepped off a slave ship for the last time.

It freed him to follow his dream of entering the ministry. To test the idea, he held dinners at home for friends. After dessert, he preached a sermon. He also studied scripture and taught himself the biblical languages Hebrew and Greek.

Newton's first diary entry about a religious vocation is dated February 1758. Soon after, he attended a prayer meeting with his faithful mentor Clunie. There, for the first time, Newton met John Wesley, the British revivalist preacher who founded the Methodist church.

Wesley suggested that Newton become a preacher, traveling from town to town. But Newton wanted to settle down, and he felt a loyalty to the Anglican tradition. Soon after that, Clunie arranged for Newton to be invited to a dinner at the home of Wesley's one-time associate George Whitefield, who also encouraged Newton.

Wesley and Whitefield were firebrand preachers. Their sermons were

JOHN WESLEY

BRITISH-BORN JOHN WESLEY AND GEORGE WHITEFIELD, BOTH ANGLICAN PRIESTS, TOURED THE EASTERN UNITED STATES PREACHING CONVERSION TO FAMILIES AND LARGE GROUPS LOOKING FOR SPIRITUAL GUIDANCE. THEY HELPED TO SPARK A RELIGIOUS REVIVAL THAT SET A SPIRITUAL TONE IN AMERICA THAT HAS LASTED FOR GENERATIONS.

packed with emotion, delivered as if on the spur of the moment. They related to common people more than the elite. Newton liked everything about their style, which was nothing like that of the typical Anglican priest.

Both preachers toured the eastern United States as well as England in the 1730s and 1740s. In England, they attracted huge crowds. Whitefield was popular in America, Wesley was not.

It was some time before Newton could adapt their ways to the Anglican tradition. His dream of the ministry did not come easily to him. To qualify, a man was expected to have an Oxford or Cambridge education and Newton was self-taught.

Finally, in 1763, he met John Thornton Dartmouth, a fellow Anglican and a member of the House of Lords who was able to convince a bishop to ordain Newton. Later that year, with Lord Dartmouth's help, Newton was named the curate of Olney parish in Buckinghamshire, north of London. He and Polly moved into the vicarage on May 26, 1764.

From the first year of his ministry, Newton dared to be his own brand of clergyman. He did not imitate the intellectual and aloof Anglican priests who were the model of his day. Instead, he developed a style greatly influenced by that of his many Methodist friends.

Most clerics wore their religious habits, even when they were riding for sport. Newton wore his old seaman's jacket. Few clergymen mingled with their parishioners, preferring their libraries instead. Newton made frequent house calls, often singing hymns with the families he visited. His peculiarities won followers. After one year at Olney, the church building had to be expanded to accommodate parishioners.

In 1765 the celebrated poet William Cowper came to visit. He had read Newton's published autobiography and wanted to talk about it. Soon after, Cowper moved to Newton's parish. They began writing hymns for the congregation to sing at weekly religious gatherings in Newton's house. These hymns were published in *Olney Hymns* (1779). Among them was Newton's single eternal flame, "Amazing Grace." His lyrics were probably sung to the tune of "New Britain," another popular hymn of the era.

GEORGE WHITEFIELD

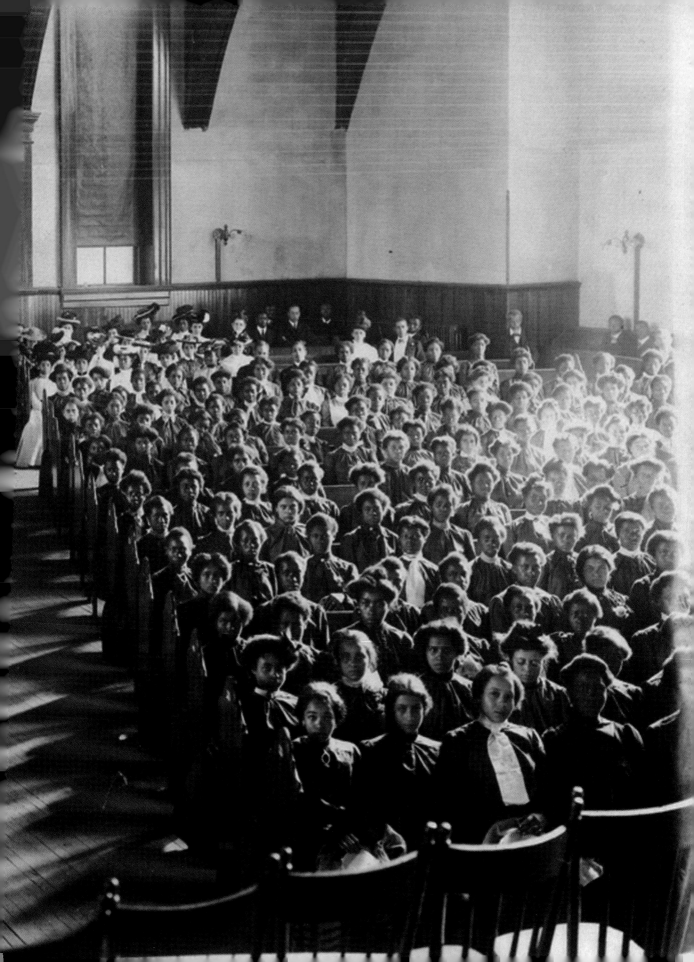

In 1779, after fifteen years at Olney, Newton was named rector of the prestigious London parish St. Mary Woolnoth. From the first week he spoke out against slavery from the pulpit. It was as if the grace he needed to face his own mistake came at the time when it could do the most good. Members of Parliament who heard his Sunday morning sermons were influenced by his words. He spoke openly of his own regrets for supporting an inhumane system. When his friend George Whitefield offered him an honorary doctorate from the University of New Jersey in America, Newton refused, saying he could only accept such a symbol of advanced learning from the Africans he had once abused.

In 1785 a powerful member of Parliament came to visit. William Wilberforce, known to be a godly man, took up the topic of abolition with Newton. From then on, the two men fought together to abolish the slave trade. Two years later Newton wrote *Thoughts on the African Slave Trade* and in it made the bravest and most complete confession of his regretted past.

"I am bound to take shame to myself by a public confession, which, however sincere, comes too late to prevent or repair the misery and mischief to which I have formerly been an accessory." Abolitionists printed three thousand copies and distributed them throughout the country. The following year, in 1788, Newton testified against the slave trade before the Privy Council.

Soon after, Polly died. She had been in frail health for some years. Their love was strong until the end. One of his last letters to her begins, "My dear, sweet, precious, beautiful own dearest dear."

Newton lived long enough to see slavery abolished in England, which was a grace in itself. He was eighty-two, his dear Polly dead seventeen years, his own health failing. He was deaf and nearly blind. He had preached his last sermon in October 1806. When he died on December 21, 1807, his friends copied down his last words, expecting that one day he would be famous: "My memory is nearly gone. But I remember two things; that I am a great sinner, and that Christ is a great savior."

Not many years after he died, "Amazing Grace" lived in the hearts of Americans.

PART III

GRACE IN AMERICA

'TWAS GRACE THAT TAUGHT MY HEART TO FEAR, AND GRACE MY FEARS RELIEVED

EVEN before "Amazing Grace" was written in England, Jonathan Edwards was helping to prepare the way for its popularity in America. He was a Calvinist preacher and one of the leaders in the Great Awakening, the religious revival movement of the mid-1700s that sprang from New England soil. Like Newton, he saw that God showered gifts on all His people. But Edwards fervently believed that heaven-sent grace was poured out on a particularly favored land, and that land was America.

Awestruck by the bounty and abundance of this country, Edwards saw it as a place alive with the Holy Spirit. "When God is about to turn the world into a paradise, he begins in the wilderness," he exclaimed.

He preached that America would be the site of the millennium, the thousand-year period mentioned in the Book of Revelation when God's kingdom would take up residence on earth. The glowing descriptions of the new heaven and the new earth in scripture, where justice would prevail and all would have

EVEN BEFORE THE REVOLUTION, COLONISTS SHARED A CONVICTION THAT GOD SHOWERED
HEAVEN-SENT GRACE ON A PARTICULARLY FAVORED LAND, AND THAT LAND WAS AMERICA.

everything they needed, were his inspiration. It was his personal interpretation of the scriptures that made America the site of this paradise.

To prepare for this future, he preached "the good society," or how people ought to behave in a perfect world. To begin, all Americans should return to the religious faith of their fathers and mothers. Edwards longed to restore the unquestioning attitudes of his own Puritan ancestors. He had no patience for a growing trend toward skeptical thinking about religion. He felt that the mystery of divinity should not be dissected as if it were a science. He worried that the Enlightenment, the European intellectual movement filtering into the colonies, could shake a person's faith. Rather than analyzing the ways of the divine, he advocated the sort of emotional surrender to God that Newton would later describe in his hymn.

After he graduated from Yale College in 1720 at seventeen, Edwards settled in Massachusetts and began preaching his message. Edwards quickly found an audience among evangelical preachers who followed a conservative doctrine, who built their relationship with God on a heartfelt spiritual conversion and who spread their faith with rousing enthusiasm. His reputation grew in England, where John Wesley read and admired his essays, as well as at home.

The "good society" he envisioned would require the conversion of hearts. Once renewed, every heart would find it easier to live in harmony and help others along. His ideal future included a special place for political leaders. Their role was to put aside personal gain and work for the benefit of the community. Those who used the country's riches exclusively for their own profit were not fit to lead, he believed. That included the British, who ruled America at the time.

Edwards' view was shared by many colonists. They believed that the British who controlled the country threatened to reduce America to the status of a mere possession, to be emptied of its treasure for the sake of England's gain. This system stifled America's growth, since it imposed British goods on the colonists, boosting England's economy at America's expense.

Edwards all but openly called for a revolt against this system, albeit on religious grounds. He believed that independent rule was essential if America was

REV. JONA. EDWARDS.

Jonathan Edwards

to realize his millennial vision. For the good society to flourish, it must rule itself, he insisted. "The art of navigation [commercial trade] used so much by wicked debauched men, shall then be consecrated to God and applied to holy uses," he wrote of the perfect future.

His words, and those of like-minded preachers, were heard. It was a brief thirty years from the height of the Great Awakening to the start of the American Revolution.

By the turn of the nineteenth century, American artists had taken up Edwards' inspiring theme. They saw this country as a blessed wilderness, lovely as paradise. A group of landscape painters known as the Hudson River school captured scenes from nature, showing the country's lush, virginal beauty. In the

8870: Gateway Rocks, Garden of the Gods,
Colorado Springs, Colo.

1830s Asher B. Durand, a leader of the movement, painted a view of the Hudson River valley in which it resembled a heavenly garden. Over the next fifty years, artists such as Albert Bierstadt and Thomas Moran moved their easels from the studio to the open air. They climbed the Adirondack mountains, hiked the Grand Canyon and camped by California mountain lakes. There they painted natural vistas as romantic visions. As the century progressed, a second group of painters, known as the Luminists, took the idea further. By the 1870s, this outgrowth of the Hudson River school had transformed New England coastline and farmlands into shimmering, mystical visions.

In the nineteenth century, American photographers also traveled the country, recording natural wonders. They captured the majesty of their subjects as if they were photographing religious monuments. (The practice continued well into the twentieth century, when Ansel Adams became perhaps the best-known keeper of the tradition. He portrayed Yosemite National Park and the deserts of the American west in ways that conveyed his own reverence for the land.)

American pioneers and explorers, too, felt their land was blessed by God. They chose Biblical names for many of America's mountains, valleys, towns and territories. Mount Zion, now part of a national park in Utah, is a classic of its kind. It was named by Mormons who settled nearby in the 1860s, to honor the hill in Jerusalem where King David built his city dedicated to God.

As the idea of America as a chosen land gained popularity through the nineteenth century, so did Newton's hymn. It is not certain exactly when "Amazing Grace" first appeared in this country. Some believe it was published here as early as 1789. A Methodist hymnbook of 1829 shows that "Amazing Grace" was included at outdoor religious gatherings, where thousands of people met to pray and sing. These rousing, rallylike events were modeled on those George Whitefield, the British revivalist preacher Newton so admired, staged during his sweep through eastern America almost a century earlier. The title of the Methodist hymnal tells the tale: *Zion Songster, A Collection of Hymns and Spiritual Songs Generally Sung at Camp and Prayer Meetings, and in Revivals of Religion*. The words inspire images of summer evenings in woodsy clearings and

TABERNACLE ORGAN AND CHOIR,
SALT LAKE CITY, UTAH.

Drawn on Stone by E.W. Clay.

METHODIST

CAMP MEETING.

WHEN THE COUNTRY WAS
STILL YOUNG, REVIVAL
PREACHERS ADVOCATED
THAT AMERICANS RETURN
TO THE UNQUESTIONING
FAITH OF THEIR FATHERS
AND MOTHERS. THEY
HOPED TO INSPIRE THE
SAME SORT OF EMOTIONAL
SURRENDER TO GOD THAT
NEWTON DESCRIBED IN
"AMAZING GRACE."

of baptisms in nearby rivers.

Edwards' view of America as God's chosen land echoed sacred scripture, in which God's own people, the Israelites, claimed Canaan was their promised home. Rooted in the teachings of John Calvin, Edwards' concept of a society built on brotherly and sisterly love was a comforting thought to his followers, as well.

Calvin is best known as a leader of the Protestant Reformation in the sixteenth century. But he was also governor of Geneva, Switzerland, where he organized the city according to his code of ethics. There was no privileged class in his system. Office holders came from the people, and every citizen was expected to take an active part in civic affairs. In these ways, he believed, society could

MT. BAKER CREVASSE

GARDEN OF THE GODS, COLORADO.

5332. The Great Augusta Natural Bridge, Utah
One of the Scenic Wonders of the World

resemble the heavenly City of God.

Edwards, like most leaders of America's Great Awakening, was a professed Calvinist. Newton was, too, but within limits. Calvin believed that the chosen ones receive God's saving grace, but not all are chosen. Newton preached that everyone has access to salvation. What is more, he favored dancing and general merry-making, far more than a pure Calvinist would. "There are slights, niceties and hard sayings to be found among some Calvinists which I do not choose to imitate," Newton wrote.

As history proves, the canopy of grace that Edwards saw arching over America was not impenetrable. It could be torn and damaged. No event in the nation's history brought that home more powerfully than the Civil War. Suddenly, America was paradise lost — lost and confused, and deeply wounded. This was a terrible break from the long decades of peace and prosperity.

President Abraham Lincoln alluded to a change that came over America during its pre-war years of bounty and good fortune. "Intoxicated with unbroken success, we have become too self-sufficient to feel the necessity of redeeming and preserving grace," he wrote, "too proud to pray to the God that made us."

Finally, the grace Lincoln hoped for did come. It was an awesome encounter not unlike Newton's own on the stormy sea. The Civil War era's "The Battle Hymn of the Republic," with lyrics by Julia Ward Howe, describes the moment in fearsome detail:

> Mine eyes have seen the glory of the coming of the Lord
> He is trampling out the vintage where the grapes of wrath are stored
> He hath loosed the fateful lightning of His terrible swift sword
> His truth is marching on.

The Civil War was indeed a moment of truth. After it, America needed to expand its understanding of the word *grace*. Always, grace contains truth. In Lincoln's time it was a terrible truth. The injustice of slavery, weighed against its economic advantages, was an issue that threatened the nation's claim to democracy.

10551 SAVING SINNERS, SCENE ALONG THE MISSISSIPPI

Grace struck the favored nation and nearly ripped it apart. As a result of the war, slavery was outlawed, but poverty and unemployment followed. Binding up the nation's wounds was a slow process, leaving ample time to contemplate the awesome grace that had enforced freedom. This is the sort of painful blessing that Newton describes in the second verse of his hymn. Grace taught the nation's heart to fear.

The Civil War song recalls Newton's hymn in another sense as well. "The Battle Hymn of the Republic" became a spiritual for all Americans. Well into the twentieth century, children of every religious background learned it in school. Many still consider it part of their American heritage. To some extent, by embracing one hymn as a national spiritual, the country was prepared to accept others. "Amazing Grace" was destined for the same place in America's heart.

It took some time to recover, but the country's identity as a blessed

place did not die with the Civil War. "America the Beautiful," whose lyrics were written in 1892 by Katharine Lee Bates, praised the bounty and beauty of the land and credited it to one source: "America! America! God shed His grace on thee." By the mid-1900s, it had become another of the nation's secular spirituals, thanks in part to popular singer Kate Smith, who sang it during her television appearances in the 1950s.

By then, "Amazing Grace" had come closer to the sphere of the national spiritual. In 1947 gospel singer Mahalia Jackson helped move it toward anthem stature when she recorded it. Her version of the hymn was often played on the radio to comfort the country as it continued to recover from the losses of World War II. Jackson helped bring "Amazing Grace" into the mainstream.

In the 1960s Martin Luther King Jr. brought the hymn to greater public attention when he and his associates sang it as they led civil rights marches. In particular, King's faithful co-worker Fannie Lou Hamer called on the hymn quite often. For years, public demonstrations and marches supporting the movement filled the nightly news. Millions of Americans heard the hymn along with King's message of equal rights for people of every race and color. He preached on the subject with passion and a fervent faith that change would come.

And as change did come, he celebrated each hard-won step with hope. King reflected on those grace-filled moments when black men and women acted on their legal right to dine in any public place, sit in any seat on a public bus, send their children to better schools. And he kept them in mind as he prepared his inspirational sermons. In one, "Our God Is Able," delivered to his Baptist congregation in the early 1960s, King suggested the cost of his courage.

"Admitting the weighty problems and staggering disappointments, Christianity affirms that God is able to give us the power to meet them," he began.

King went on to describe anonymous phone calls that threatened his life. He described the bomb blast that destroyed his family's home. Mercifully, no family member was hurt. He described a sleepless night just before that bombing. "I was ready to give up," he declared. Sitting at his kitchen table, head in hands, he prayed. "I am at the end of my powers. I have nothing left. I've come to the

point where I can't face it alone.

"At that moment I experienced the presence of the Divine as I had never before experienced Him. It seemed as though I could hear the quiet assurance of an inner voice saying, 'Stand up for righteousness, stand up for truth. God will be at your side forever.' Almost at once, my fears began to pass from me."

The winds of grace are always blowing. King showed us what it means to open our sails even when we are filled with fear. The grace that came to him at that time restored his inner peace.

In the early 1970s, near the end of the Vietnam war, Judy Collins recorded "Amazing Grace." Her version captured the melancholy and regret shared by many Americans who felt that too many lives had been lost in a war many believed the U.S. could not win.

It was Collins who firmly placed Newton's hymn in the realm of the

The Lord has promised good to me,
His word my hope secures.
He will my shield and portion be
As long as life endures.

secular spiritual. Within a few weeks of its release, "everyone knew the song, it seemed, and wanted to hear it," she wrote in her book titled after the hymn.

She remembered learning the hymn as a girl attending Methodist church services. Once she recorded it, people requested it at concerts. Everyone sang it with her at the end of the evening, as a sort of prayer. She has described singing Newton's hymn as a mystical experience and a profound spiritual communion.

In the years since Collins recorded it, the country often has turned to the hymn in moments when we have all been at a loss for words.

In 1986, after the space shuttle *Challenger* burst into flames before the nation's eyes, religious leaders reflected on the tragic loss. "People . . . realize how fragile life is and how quickly it can be snuffed out," said the Reverend Billy Graham. In the future, he suggested, Americans might be more concerned for the safety of all astronauts. "It will cause us, when we watch their launch, to say a prayer for their safety. We've taken it for granted for so long." The prayers and eulogies of the memorial service for the *Challenger* astronauts were powerfully echoed when "Amazing Grace" was played.

And in 1995, when terrorists detonated a bomb at an Oklahoma City federal building and killed 168 people, congregations around the country prayed together for the victims and their families. Television news cameras covered these services, and we heard "Amazing Grace" across the land.

These tragedies, shared by all the nation, remind us of the truth that we humans find so painful to accept. We do not control the world, and that fills us with fear. As King described the feeling, "I am at the end of my powers. I have nothing left. I've come to the point where I can't face it alone."

In the same sermon, King remembered how he looked beyond that painful place and found the creator of heaven and earth. He described this vision of God in cosmic terms. "Before we are consumed too greatly by our man-made arrogance," he advised, "let us take a broader look at the universe. . . . In the past seven minutes we have been hurtled more than eight thousand miles through space." He pointed out that the earth moves at the rate of 66,700 miles per hour. He pointed out that it revolves around a sun that seems very near but is ninety-

three million miles away. Still, he reminded us, our earth will travel past that sun and we will be on the other side of it in just six months.

The maker of the cosmos holds us up when we feel as if our world is falling down. At our weakest, said King, "we are forced to look beyond man and affirm anew that God is able."

The hymn we so often turn to brings the same message of hope. We sing it, and we remember that our God is able.

Through many dangers, toils and snares I have already come.

'Tis grace has brought me safe thus far, And grace will lead me home.

BIBLIOGRAPHY

WORKS BY JOHN NEWTON

Cecil, Richard. *The Works of Rev. John Newton: To Which Are Pre-fixed Memoirs of His Life*. Edinburgh: Thomas Nelson, 1840.

Newton, John. *Journal of a Slave Trader*. Introduction by Bernard Martin and Mark Spurrell. London: Epworth Press, 1962.

Newton, John. *The Progress of Grace in Three Letters to a Friend*. London: date unknown.

Newton, John. *Olney Hymns in Three Books*. New York: Everett Duyckinck, 1808.

BIOGRAPHIES OF JOHN NEWTON

Martin, Bernard. *John Newton, A Biography*. London: William Heinemann Ltd., 1950.

Martin, Bernard. *John Newton and the Slave Trade*. London: Congmans, Green & Co, Ltd., 1960.

Pollock, John. *Amazing Grace: John Newton's Story*. New York: Harper & Row, 1981.

AMERICAN RELIGIOUS HISTORY

Ahlstrom, Sydney E. *A Religious History of the American People*. New Haven: Yale University Press, 1972.

Gaustad, Edwin Scott. *The Great Awakening in New England*. Chicago: Quadrangle, 1957.

Heimert, Alan. *Religion and the American Mind, From the Great Awakening to the Revolution*. Cambridge: Harvard University Press, 1966.

AMERICAN ART HISTORY

Novak, Barbara. *American Painting of the Nineteenth Century*. New York: Praeger, 1969.

Wilmerding, John, editor, with contributions by Lisa Andrus, et al. *American Light; the Luminist Movement, 1850-1875: Paintings, Drawings, Photographs*. Washington, D.C.: National Gallery of Art, 1980.

GENERAL INTEREST

Colson, Charles. *Born Again*. Grand Rapids: Spire Books, 1976.

King, Martin Luther, Jr. *Strength to Love*. Philadelphia: Fortress Press, 1963.

VIDEOTAPES

Moyers, Bill. *Amazing Grace With Bill Moyers*. Newbridge Communications, 1994.

ILLUSTRATION AND PHOTOGRAPH CREDITS

Unless otherwise noted here, all photographs and ephemeral materials are from private collections. While every effort has been made to trace all present copyright holders of the material in this book, any unintentional omission is hereby apologized for in advance. The authors will be pleased to correct any acknowledgment errors or omissions in future editions of *Amazing Grace in America*.

Book jacket and page 8: LONGWOOD GARDEN PARTY, 1919
Hagley Museum and Library
Wilmington, Delaware

page vii: EMMA KICKAPOO, UNIDENTIFIED TRIBE
Negative No. 316978, courtesy
Department of Library Services
American Museum of Natural History, New York City

page 13: MARIAN ANDERSON ON THE STEPS OF THE LINCOLN MEMORIAL, WASHINGTON, D.C., 1939
UPI/Corbis-Bettmann, New York City

page 15: SKATING IN SUN VALLEY
Union Pacific Railroad Photo

pages 18-19, 25: Courtesy of the American Bible Society, New York City

pages 26-27: HOME OF SYLVESTER RAWDING FAMILY, NORTH OF WEST UNION, CUSTER COUNTY, NEBRASKA, 1886
Solomon D. Butcher Collection
Nebraska State Historical Society

page 31: Bottom, L'ANGELUS, Jean-Francois Millet

page 33: Courtesy of the American Bible Society, New York City

page 43: DRAWING OF JOHN NEWTON, Russell Pinx
Reproduced from the Collections of the Library of Congress

pages 44-45: BRIGOON "HERALD" OFF DINCORE, AFRICA
Courtesy of Peabody Essex Museum
Salem, Massachusetts

pages 48-49: MAP OF AFRICA, 1573
G. Lolivier, Paris

page 51: Top, courtesy of the American Bible Society, New York City; bottom, PRAYING HANDS, Albrecht Dürer, 1508.

pages 52-53: DIAGRAM: SLAVE SHIP PLAN
Manuscripts, Archives and Rare Books Division
Schomburg Center for Research in Black Culture
The New York Public Library
Astor, Lenox and Tilden Foundations

page 56: NEGROES JUST LANDED FROM A SLAVE SHIP, 1808, engraving by W. Ralph
Print Collection, Miriam and Ira D. Wallach Division of Arts, Prints and Photographs
The New York Public Library
Astor, Lenox and Tilden Foundations

page 57: **SLAVE TRADE POSTER**
Reproduced from the Collections of the
Library of Congress

page 59: **THE VOYAGE OF THE SABLE VENUS**
Etching and engraving by W. Granger, after
Thomas Stothard, extra-illustrated edition
of Bray's *Life of Thomas Stothard*,
(London: 1851)
Print Collection, Miriam and Ira D. Wallach
Division of Arts, Prints and Photographs
The New York Public Library
Astor, Lenox and Tilden Foundations

page 67: **PAPER OF JOHN NEWTON**
Manuscript Division. Department of
Rare Books and Special Collections
Princeton University Libraries

pages 68-69: **LA GARDEUSE**, Jean-Francois
Millet

pages 72-73: **BAPTISM IN KENTUCKY**, 1949
Reproduced from the Collections of the
Library of Congress

page 79: **GEORGE WHITEFIELD**
Reproduced from the Collections of the
Library of Congress

pages 80-81: **TUSKEGEE INSTITUTE
CHAPEL, ALABAMA**, 1903
Photograph by Frances B. Johnston
Reproduced from the Collections of the
Library of Congress

page 83: **HOPE**, G.F. Watts

page 85: **KINDRED SPIRITS**, Asher B. Durand.
Oil on canvas. 1849
Collection of the New York Public Library
Astor, Lenox and Tilden Foundations

page 89: **JONATHAN EDWARDS**
Reproduced from the Collections of the
Library of Congress

page 91: **GEOLOGICAL FORMATIONS**, Gallatin
National Forest, Montana, 1926
U.S. Forest Service

pages 98-99: **METHODIST CAMP
MEETING**, 1836
Harry T. Peters "America on Stone"
Lithography Collection
Smithsonian Institution

page 100: Courtesy of the American
Bible Society

page 101: **RIVER BAPTISM**
State Historical Society of Wisconsin

page 105: Top, **LINCOLN READS THE
EMANCIPATION PROCLAMATION**, 1864
Reproduced from the Collections of the
Library of Congress; bottom, **AN AFRICAN
SLAVE MARKET**, painting by Taylor, 1852.
Chicago Historical Society

page 106: **NURSE WITH HER "CHARGE"**
Harbell, 1899
Reproduced from the Collections of the
Library of Congress

page 107: Top left, **SAMUEL CROWTHER**
Courtesy of the American Bible Society

page 111: Courtesy of the American
Bible Society

page 114-115: **DR. MARTIN LUTHER KING LEADS
CIVIL RIGHTS MARCHERS FROM SELMA TO
MONTGOMERY, ALABAMA, ON MARCH 3, 1965**
UPI/Corbis-Bettmann, New York City

page 118: **SILENT PARADE, JULY 28, 1917,
FIFTH AVENUE, NEW YORK CITY**
Photographs and Prints Division
Schomburg Center for Research in
Black Culture
The New York Public Library
Astor, Lenox and Tilden Foundations

Angel City Press, established in 1992, is dedicated to
the publication of high-quality nonfiction gift books.
Angel City Press is located by the sea in
Santa Monica, California.